Old Mother Goose

A ZEBRA BOOK
Illustrated by Elizabeth Wood

PUBLISHED BY

WALKER BOOKS
LONDON

Old Mother Goose,

When she wanted to wander,

Would ride through the air

On a very fine gander.

Mother Goose had a house,

'Twas built in a wood,

Where an owl at the door

For sentinel stood.

She had a son Jack,
A plain-looking lad,
He was not very good,
Nor yet very bad.

She sent him to market,
A live goose he bought;
See, mother, says he,
I have not been for nought.

Jack's goose and her gander
Grew very fond;
They'd both eat together,
Or swim in the pond.

Jack found one fine morning,

As I have been told,

His goose had laid him

An egg of pure gold.

Jack ran to his mother
The news for to tell,
She called him a good boy,
And said it was well.

Jack sold his gold egg
To a merchant untrue,
Who cheated him out of
A half of his due.

Then Jack went a-courting

A lady so gay,

As fair as the lily,

And sweet as the May.

The merchant and squire
Soon came at his back,
And began to belabour
The sides of poor Jack.

Then old Mother Goose

That instant came in,

And turned her son Jack

Into famed Harlequin.